Tales from a
small blue planet

Steve Beal

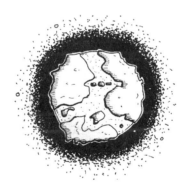

Copyright © Steve Beal 2004
First published 2004
ISBN 1 84427 004 1

Scripture Union, 207–209 Queensway, Bletchley, Milton Keynes, MK2
2EB, England.
Email: info@scriptureunion.org.uk
Website: www.scriptureunion.org.uk

Scripture Union Australia
Locked Bag 2, Central Coast Business Centre, NSW 2252
Website: www.su.org.au

Scripture Union USA
PO Box 987, Valley Forge, PA 19482
www.scriptureunion.org

Scripture quotations are from the Contemporary English Version published by HarperCollins Publishers, copyright © 1991, 1992, 1995
American Bible Society.

British Library Cataloguing-in-Publication Data.
A catalogue record of this book is available from the British Library.

Printed and bound in Great Britain by Creative Print and Design
(Wales) Ebbw Vale.

Cover design: Paul Airy
Cover and all internal illustrations: Steve Beal

Scripture Union is an international Christian charity working with
churches in more than 130 countries, providing resources to bring the
good news about Jesus Christ to children, young people and families
and to encourage them to develop spiritually through the Bible and
prayer.

As well as our network of volunteers, staff and associates who run holi-
days, church-based events and school Christian groups, we produce a
wide range of publications and support those who use our resources
through training programmes.

Contents

To Karen – a hope and a future.

Stardust

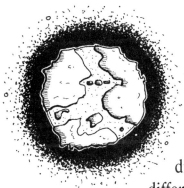

Once on a small blue planet, a long way from here, there lived people just like you and me. They may have lived in different houses and played different games, they may have eaten different food and spoken in different languages but inside they were just the same.

Now this small blue planet was closer than normal to the stars, so close in fact that on occasion, dust from those stars would fall through the sky and land twinkling on the ground. Sometimes, if you were lucky, you might be walking through the jumble bushes and see, on a flower petal, a shining speck of stardust.

The people of this small blue planet spent lots of time searching high and low, far and wide, hoping all the time to find even the tiniest speck of stardust. It wasn't the fact that it shone even in the day or that the colours were so beautiful – the real reason was that when you held the stardust in your hand something very special happened.

As you closed your hand around it a warm feeling started to grow somewhere deep inside you. The feeling grew and grew until you were warm all over and then it happened. Suddenly you remembered all the best bits of your life, all the happiness, goodness, fun and laughter, and not only that, the stardust reminded you how special you really were. Special, not because of what you had done or how much you had, but because you were you. So you can see why so much time was spent looking amongst the twizzleberries, just in case a small speck of stardust had fallen there.

One day, one of the people of the small blue planet (she was called Halbonbaltiddlyaljofal but her friends called her Hal for short) was out in

search of stardust. Like all of her people she was loaded up with all her possessions. That's the way her people liked to do things – they carried everything. When I say everything, I mean everything: all their clothes, all their bedding, all their shoes, all their special things. Hal kept all her special things in a beautiful red leather bag. People even took their not so special things everywhere, like the pink bunny suit a distant aunt had sent them for their birthday. Some people believed that

7

the more things you had, the more important you were.

Hal dreamed of finding even a tiny piece of stardust but no one had found any in such a long time and Hal had never even seen any.

Now Hal was very clever and instead of looking under the snoring stones or among the dillydaffs like the others she stopped and thought for a while.

Where can I find some stardust? Where does it come from? Where would it land? she asked herself.

She looked up to the sky and then looked all around and when she had finished thinking she knew just what to do.

Across the river was a high hill and on the high hill was a findle tree which grew higher still, higher than anything around.

That's the place, thought Hal.

With all her possessions still strapped to her back, she crossed the river and climbed the hill until she came to the base of the findle tree. It was enormous.

Even though she was already tired from scaling the hill, Hal started to climb the findle tree branch by branch, rising higher than any of her people had ever been before. Finally she reached the top of the tree. The branches were narrower here and could barely hold Hal's weight but she would not give up. Very carefully she pushed her head through the last of the findle leaves and looked around. There, not far from her, she saw a piece of stardust, not small at all, but as big as a pebble. Hal just stared. She had never seen anything so beautiful, so bright, so alive with colour. Just looking at it made her want to cry with happiness, to sing and dance and shout. Not that she did, you understand, for dancing and thin branches are not a good combination.

Eventually Hal reached out, stretching as far as she could, but she couldn't get the stardust. She climbed a little further up the ever-narrowing twigs but her weight made the branch bend further away. No matter how she tried she couldn't reach the stardust. Tears of frustration filled her eyes but she wasn't about to give in.

As we already know, Hal was very clever and

she stopped for a while and thought.

How can I reach the stardust? What can I do? she said to herself.

She looked up to the stardust and then looked all around and when she had finished thinking she knew just what to do.

Hal undid a buckle and removed a strap, and a sack of not very important things, including a ghastly pink bunny suit, fell from sight and crashed through the leaves never to be seen again. The branch moved a little closer but nowhere near enough.

Though it was hard, Hal undid some more buckles and straps and three bags of important things fell away, never to be seen again. The branch moved a little closer to the stardust, and Hal reached out, stretching her fingers as far as she could, but it was still not enough.

Though it was harder still, and not many others had ever done it, Hal undid even more straps and buckles, and two bags and a box of very important things fell through the tree never to be seen again. The branch moved a lot closer to the stardust but still Hal could not reach it.

Hal had one bag left, her beautiful red leather bag containing her most precious things. After a moment she even dropped that too, never to be seen again. The branch moved, Hal reached out as far as she could and plucked the stardust from its resting-place.

Carefully Hal climbed down the findle tree and sat with her back against the trunk, exhausted. She could not take her eyes from the shining beauty of the stardust. Carefully she closed her hand around it and felt, deep inside, a warmth that grew and grew until it filled every part of her. She started to remember all the best bits of her life, all the happiness, goodness, fun and laughter. Then she remembered how special she was, not because of what she had done or what she had had, but because she was Hal, Halbonbaltiddlyaljofal.

One of our bloopers is missing

As you may know, bloopers come in all shapes and sizes. You probably even have a favourite. Maybe the woolly blooper or the spotted blooper, maybe the giant blooper or even the big-bottomed blooper. You may also know that

bloopers gather together in herds with a mixture of every kind of blooper. If you have studied Bloopology (as I know many of you have) you will also know that each blooper makes its own sound and when mixed with the sounds of all the other bloopers, this makes music. This is no ordinary music. The music made by bloopers is soothing and calm and makes even the grouchiest person happy. It is like the first spoonful of your favourite pudding. It is like stretching in bed when you know you do not have to get up. It is like your favourite day.

But did you know that if just one blooper stops singing, the music goes wrong? It sounds almost the same but with something missing. Then it is like going on a journey and knowing you've forgotten something but not being able to work out what it is. It is like that feeling in your tummy when you first realise something has gone wrong. It is like an itch, an itch you cannot scratch.

One day El got that itch.

El looked after the bloopers. He knew them all by name, even Bo and Jo the twins, who he never got mixed up. He helped them to find snuzzleberries (a real treat for a blooper), he removed tangles from the woolly ones,  he made sure the smaller ones were not accidentally trodden on by the larger ones and sometimes he would sing to the music they made. He loved them very much.

On the day that El got that itch he was sitting on his favourite rock on the hillside above Blooperville watching the bloopers at play. He had just finished curing San, a crested blooper, of the hiccups when he noticed that something was not quite right. He looked around and there in the distance was Bloo in a place he should not be.

Bloo was a spotted blooper, a curious one at that, and sometimes he

would wander off. Most of the time it did not matter because he did not go far and always came back when El called him. But this time Bloo could smell snuzzleberries. The smell was so strong that at first Bloo thought they must be quite near. So he went a little way from the herd in search of the snuzzleberries but he couldn't find them. He crossed the stream and started to look around on the next hill but still he could not find them. At the top of the hill Bloo heard El calling his name. He knew he should go back but the snuzzleberries could not be far away and they smelt so good.

What a feast it will be, thought Bloo. He pretended not to hear El calling him.

I will just get the snuzzleberries, he thought to himself, and then I will go back.

So Bloo carried on his search, getting further and further away from the herd. Over streams and across fields he travelled, around huge trees and through small bushes. Soon he found himself at the edge of an emerald forest. The afternoon sun shone through the dancing leaves, the birds sang and the grass was soft under his feet. He looked all around but still he could not find the snuzzleberries. He searched under the jumble bushes and behind the findle trees but still nothing. The smell was very strong now and Bloo searched even deeper into the forest, and there he found it. What he found was not a snuzzleberry bush at all but a thorny snaggleberry bush. As all good Bloopologists know, snaggleberries smell a bit like snuzzleberries but they do not taste as good and they give you tummy-ache.

Maybe I should go home, thought a disappointed Bloo.

But when he looked around him all he could see was trees and their branches did not seem so pleasant now that the light was fading. He could not remember which way he had come and could not think which way to go. He was lost.

Back on the hill above Blooperville, El shouted as loud as he could, calling Bloo's name, but Bloo did not turn around. In fact, Bloo disappeared over a distant hill.

"Do not go anywhere, and stay out of trouble," said El to the rest of the herd and

with that he set off to find Bloo. When he reached the top of the hill Bloo was nowhere to be seen but El guessed he must have gone into the forest. He sniffed the air.

"Snaggleberries," he sighed.

Bloo, meanwhile, was trying to get home but no matter how he tried, he always seemed to end up back at the snaggleberry bush and now he was hungry. He looked at the snaggleberries.

Just one will not hurt, he thought – and ate three. He tried to convince himself that they were not that bad and ate five more. Soon his tummy started to hurt and he felt woozy. Bloo fell over, right into the thorny snaggleberry bush. He tried to get out but he couldn't. He was tangled in the spiky branches and the more he struggled the more tangled he got.

Why did I wander away? thought Bloo sadly, and he gave a little bloop: "Bloop!"

"There you are," said a voice.

It was El.

"Oh Bloo, you have got yourself into a real mess. Let me help."

El waded into the snaggleberry bush and though it scratched his hands and his feet, he didn't care because he loved Bloo and wanted to see him safe. Soon El had lifted Bloo from the snaggleberry bush, and gently carried him back to the herd.

When he got back he had lots to do. Two sticky bloopers had stuck together, a short-legged blooper had fallen over and could not get up, and a long-tailed blooper had a sore tail from being stood on by a (very embarrassed) big-footed blooper. El put Bloo on the ground and watched him for a while as he played with the other bloopers.

"Bloopers," said El, shaking his head. And he listened to the soothing music they made.

It won't surprise you to know that there are no bloopers in the Bible! But Jesus told a story about a sheep who was a lot like poor old Bloo. Here's what he said:

"Let me ask you this. What would you do if you had a hundred sheep and one of them wandered off? Wouldn't you leave the ninety-nine on the hillside and go and look for the one that had wandered away? I am sure that finding it would make you happier than having the ninety-nine that never wandered off."

Why did Jesus tell this story? Here's the ending:

"That's how it is with your Father in heaven. He doesn't want any of these little ones to be lost."

Just like El loved his bloopers, and a shepherd loves his sheep, God loves all of us. Don't go wandering off though!

Matthew 18:12–14

Bik and Bok

On a small moon circling the small blue planet, there lived two creatures. One was Bik and the other Bok. Some people said they were different, but that didn't even start to explain this strange pair! They were total opposites, like the chalkiest chalk and the cheesiest cheese. Like the hottest fire and the coldest ice. What one liked the other did not. What one ate the other did not. What one did the other did not.

Except...

They both loved meteor storms, huge big rocks falling out of the sky. Well, it takes all sorts! They were both members of the Intergalactic Debris In Our Time Society (IDIOTS to you and me) and each had one hundred books on the subject of meteors.

But apart from this they had nothing in common.

Bik was happy and smiley but Bok was not,
 Bik was bright yellow but Bok was not,
  Bik liked lime jelly sandwiches but Bok did not,
 Bik played the trombone but Bok did not.

It so happened that during the month of Do (the other month was called Don't) a huge meteor shower was due to light up the sky of the small moon where they lived. Never before had so many rocks fallen from the sky. This was the big one, the main event, the real deal, the unmissable, unstoppable, greatest of all – it was quite important! Bik and Bok were very excited but, of course, in very different ways.

 Bik looked for a good spot but Bok did not,
 Bik packed himself a nice lunch but Bok did not,
 Bik wore an "I love meteors" T-shirt but Bok did not,
 Bik picked a snazzy hat but Bok did not.

 And so came the day of the meteor shower. Bik set out with his lunch nice and early and

strolled to the place he had chosen on a leisurely walk the day before. He had decided that to get the best view he would climb to the top of a huge, solid rock as old as the moon itself. He climbed steadily and carefully, taking time to work out all his foot and finger holds. At the top he looked at his clockometer and found he had time for a lime jelly sandwich before the show started.

Bik was early for the show but Bok was not,

Bik was full of yummy food but Bok was not,

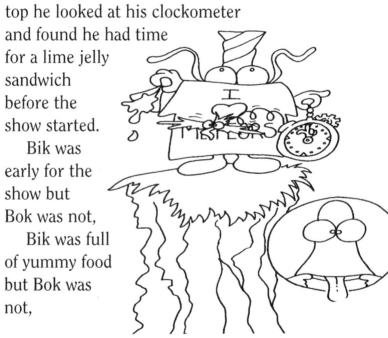

Bik was ready and relaxed but Bok was not,
Bik was enjoying his morning but Bok was not.

Bok woke up late and fell out of bed in a panic. He ran around in circles for a while until he realised that it was not getting him anywhere and then he ran outside. He ran back inside and changed out of his pink pyjamas and into some proper clothes. Then he half ran, half walked, trying to tie his shoelace on the move. Not a good idea unless you like falling down a lot. He completely forgot his hat, his coat and his food.

Bik was playing the trombone but Bok was not,

Bik was watching the sky but Bok was not,
Bik had lots of time but Bok did not,
Bik was ready but Bok was not.

At the last minute Bok arrived at the site. He was tired, hungry and generally discombobulated*. He looked up to where Bik was happily waiting; it looked like a good place. It looked solid,

27

reliable and had a great view. He looked down to where he stood. It was muddy and he could not see a lot. But Bok stayed where he was. He couldn't be bothered to climb the rock – it was too much effort.

"It will be just as good from here," he said to himself sulkily, but he didn't really believe it. He knew the rock was the best place to be.

On top of the rock Bik started to count down.

"10, 9, 8…"

In the mud Bok was shrinking. At least, that's what it felt like. He looked down. He wasn't shrinking, he was sinking. Right up to his knees.

"7, 6, 5..."
Right up to his waist.

"4, 3, 2..."
Right up to his neck.

"1!"

Bok sank completely into the sticky mud, making a tiny shloop sound as he did.

Bik watched the biggest meteor shower ever but Bok did not,

Bik saw the sky turn orange, crimson, and pink but Bik did not,

Bik jumped up and down with joy but Bok did not,

Bik was as happy as could be but Bok... well, Bok was not.

Preparing for things can sometimes be booooring but for Bik it meant he had a great time while Bok, well, Bok did not. There's another story about two people who were a bit like Bik and Bok. Jesus said:

"Anyone who hears and obeys these teachings of mine is like a wise person who built a house on solid rock. Rain poured down, rivers flooded, and winds beat against that house. But it did not fall, because it was built on solid rock.

Anyone who hears my teachings and doesn't obey them is like a foolish person who built a house on sand. The rain poured down, the rivers flooded, and the winds blew and beat against that house. Finally, it fell with a crash."

Matthew 7:24–27

The race

Welcome race lovers to the fifteenth annual groundling race... and have we got an exciting competition for you! Four, yes four, of the fastest groundlings the planet has ever seen. Hold on to your hats and brace yourselves for what is sure to be the race to end all races.

As usual the course covers a variety of difficult terrain. There is woodland, with its thorns and brambles and the occasional angry

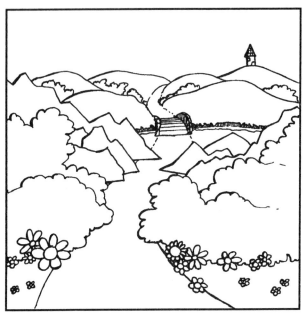

squirrel, there are rocky hills baked in the midday sun, and fast-flowing streams waiting for the unwary. Only the fittest, most dedicated groundlings are in with a chance of winning. Let's look at this year's competitors.

In the green and yellow, from the planet Bob, it's Beaky. Beaky is no stranger to racing and is a planet champion three years in a row. Watch out for a burst of speed at the beginning of the race.

In red and orange, recently recovered from an ingrowing toenail, it's Pebble. She has a lot of fans here today. She is a cool customer and seems to be at the height of her physical fitness.

Looking menacing in black, the favourite here today... Spike. He is a tough character and sure to make an impression. Look at what he's wearing, the latest in Hi-tech sportswear with the new Dynamo™ high performance running shoes. Finally, in the yellow, a relative newcomer to racing. A big round of applause for Izzy! Although ranked an outsider, keep an eye out for him – in the groundling race you just never know.

The groundlings are coming up to the line; a few last minute stretches and they are ready. The atmosphere here is electric. They are under starter's orders. They're off!

They are all together as they round the first bend but Beaky is starting to edge forward with the early speed he is known for. Over the stone bridge and up Billy Goat Lane and there is still not much in it, though Izzy is falling back slightly. Pebble looks relaxed and Spike even has time to give the cameras a winning smile – his sponsors will be pleased at that. Remember, Dynamo™ sportswear is available from all good outlets across the Milky Way.

Into the woods now and… what's this? Beaky is slowing down. What is going on? Is

he injured? This is a surprising development. The others are all past him now and he is almost at a complete standstill. He seems to be looking at something in the undergrowth. It appears to be a tiny bird. What is he doing? Has he forgotten there's a race on? Now he's feeding the bird. He has taken off his shoes. He has completely forgotten about the race and the others are way out in front. Ladies and gentlemen, the race has ended even before it has begun for Beaky.

We rejoin the others as they come out of the woods. Spike has a clear lead, Pebble is in second place and bringing up the rear with a steady pace is Izzy. They all seem to have outdistanced the pack of angry squirrels but

Izzy has taken quite a pelting from a barrage of acorns. As they approach the rocky hills, the path ends and they start to scramble over the stones and boulders. This is a hard part of the course and you can see the strain on all the competitors' faces. Spike has a clear advantage here with his Dynamo™ shoes and their built-in anti-shock cushions. Pebble seems to be struggling with this part of the course and Izzy overtakes her, going into second place. Pebble is slowing, slowing… ladies and gentlemen, Pebble has stopped. She is lying down on one of the bigger rocks. She is reaching for something… I don't believe it! Pebble has got out her sunglasses and is reading the newspaper. She's obviously had enough, it has got too tough for her and she has given up. Her fans will be very disappointed.

Further up the course, Spike has a commanding lead over Izzy, who's still keeping that steady pace. Just the streams to go and it looks like Spike is going to be an easy winner here today.
He is at
the first

stream and he has stopped. He
does not seem to want to
go into the water!
Meanwhile Izzy is gaining.
Spike is walking up and
down the bank; maybe
the water is too deep.
Izzy reaches the first
stream and runs
right through
and he is in the
lead. It seems
that Spike does not

want to get his new Dynamo™ running shoes
wet and muddy! Izzy runs through the last
stream and turns into the home straight.
Spike will not cross the stream and is sitting
by the thorn bushes looking very sorry for
himself. The race ends right there for him.
He's obviously too worried about getting his
kit messy to finish the race.

Here comes Izzy, still with that steady pace.
He crosses the line. Izzy is the winner, the
only one to complete the race. Well done, Izzy!

I can safely say that this was one of the
most controversial races of recent years. Later
we will be talking to the groundlings about
how they felt the race went. First we go over

live to the planet Bob where our reporter Grimmly Moonwalk is waiting to update us on all the action from today's Zero Gravity Tiddlywink Tournament.

Hector

Remember well dear reader
The tale I have to tell,
The story of Hector
And the things he had to sell.

You could buy all you wanted
Any colour, any style
As long as what you wanted
Was a grouchy crocodile.

They came in many sizes
Starting off with BIG,
One could ride a bicycle
Another wore a wig.

One loved to eat jelly
Another played a tune
One ate bananas
With a silver sugar spoon.

What a cool collection
What a marvellous thing
Hector took his beasties
For a visit to the king.

The king said he would like one
A blue one... with pink spots
To help his castle cooks and chefs
To wash up all the pots.

And another for the dusting
And two to make the tea
All the palace gardening
Would need another three.

But while the king was talking
Hector lost his grip
And all the toothy reptiles
Gave old Hec the slip.

Oh what mayhem followed
What turmoil did ensue
As twenty-three crocodiles
Looked for stuff to chew.

They ate the king's jam doughnuts
They bit his servants too
And they chased the animals
From the king's own private zoo.

The king's guards were called out
The cavalry were too
And of those chewing beasties
They captured twenty-two.

But one remained uncaptured
And with a great big bump
Knocked the good king over
And bit him on the rump.

The king's men were so angry
"Lock Hector up!" cried they.
"And throw away the key, right now!
In prison he must stay!"

But the king who soon recovered
Looked Hector in the eye
And said, "Hector, I forgive you
We'll let this one slide by."

Hec could not believe it
His face was sad and pale
He was sure that his pets and he
Would end their days in jail.

But no, no, no, the king was kind –
Sent Hector home for tea.
And happily they caught the croc
(Number twenty-three.)

When Hector got home that night
And entered his nice house
He found he had a visitor
A little country mouse.

The mouse was very hungry
And also very poor
And was about to eat a tiny crumb
That had fallen on the floor.

Hector began shouting
"There's a robber in my house!"
And twenty-three fierce crocodiles
Went after that poor mouse.

They chased it round the kitchen
Up the stairs and down
And finally they caught it
And pinned it to the ground.

Hector picked it up
Its eyes were wide with fear
"It's the end for you, my little friend!"
He had a wicked sneer.

But at that very moment
The door opened with a crack
And there stood the king
With his jailer at his back.

"Hector, I forgave you
And this is how you act
You're going to jail this minute
And you know that that's a fact!"

Hector spent his days in jail
His head against the bars
And twenty-three fierce crocodiles
Were his prison guards.

And if one day you see the king
Look closely and you'll see
A tiny mouse by his side
Finishing his tea.

Jesus said:

"This story will show you what the kingdom of heaven is like:

One day a king decided to call in his officials and ask them to give an account of what they owed him. As he was doing this, one official was brought in who owed him fifty million silver coins. But he didn't have any money to pay what he owed. The king ordered him to be sold, along with his wife and children and all he owned, in order to pay the debt.

The official got down on his knees and began begging, 'Have pity on me, and I will pay you every penny I owe!' The king felt sorry for him and let him go free. He even told the official that he did not have to pay back the money.

As the official was leaving, he happened to meet another official, who owed him a hundred silver coins. So he grabbed the man by the throat. He started choking him and said, 'Pay me what you owe!'

The man got down on his knees and began begging, 'Have pity on me, and I will pay you back.' But the first official refused to have pity. Instead, he went and had the other official put in jail until he could pay what he owed.

When some other officials found out what had happened, they felt sorry for the man who had been put in jail. Then they told the king what had happened. The king called the first official back in and said, 'You're an evil man! When you begged for mercy, I said you did not have to pay back a penny. Don't you think you should show pity to someone else, as I did to you?' The king was so angry that he ordered the official to be tortured until he could pay back everything he owed. That is how my Father in heaven will treat you, if you don't forgive each of my followers with all your heart."

Matthew 18:23–35

The Wozat

The desert of Khamoon is a vast stretch of
sun-scorched sand. You could walk in any
direction for six weeks and still not see
anything except sand. There is very little water
and very little life and lots and lots of sand.

In this unfriendly place live several tribes,
keeping alive by moving from one watering
hole to another. One of these tribes is called
the Stargatherers.

The Stargatherers make their homes in tents of all shapes and sizes. Each tent has bright blue, star-speckled banners outside to show which tribe they belong to. Inside they are lit with coloured lanterns

of red, orange, green and purple, and beautiful patterned rugs adorn the floor. Everything in the camp is made by the Stargatherers, from pots and tools to clothes and shoes. Everyone has a job to do from the youngest to the oldest. Nothing is wasted.

Living in one of the large tents with her family is Gem. Gem's job each day is to look after the goats. It is a very important job because the goats provide milk and meat and skins to make clothes and tents. She does not have very much that she can call her own, but she does have one special thing.

When she was much younger her great-grandmother had given her a small silver box with a carving of a tree on the lid. Her grandmother had to explain what a tree was because Gem had never seen one and she was amazed that such a thing could exist.

As her great-grandmother had given her the box she had said, "Look after this, child. One day it will be very important."

Gem did not really understand what her great-grandmother meant but she had excitedly opened the box. At first she had thought it was empty but when she concentrated and looked really hard, she could make out a tiny speck of something.

"When everything else has gone, use this," whispered her great-grandmother. "You will know when."

Gem trusted her great-grandmother and had kept the box safe.

She called the thing inside the Wozat because when people first saw it they said, "Wozat?"

Even though it was the tiniest thing she had ever seen, she kept it safe. She kept it safe because her great-grandmother had given it to her. She kept it safe because she trusted her great-grandmother had given her something special. But most of all she kept it safe because she believed the Wozat was important and that one day the Stargatherers would need it.

Some people said it wasn't real and that she was just making it up. Gem thought that maybe they weren't looking hard enough or maybe they just did not want to see it. Other people could see the Wozat but said it was useless. What could be done with something so tiny? Gem didn't know but she knew the Wozat could do something. Even though she could not prove it, deep inside, she just knew.

Then, one ordinary day, disaster struck the Stargatherers.

A huge sandstorm from the east hit the camp without warning. The winds ripped apart

the tents and blew them away. The stinging
sand got into the people's eyes and ears and
noses, and they stumbled around trying to find
shelter. The animals ran off, the water bags
burst and all the food was ruined.

After many hours the storm died away and
the Stargatherers were left scattered and
confused.

Gem lay curled in a ball, covered in sand.
Her hands and feet were sore from the
scratching sand and she was very hungry and

very thirsty. She got unsteadily to her feet and looked around. All that was left of the camp was a few scraps of material and broken pottery.

The people started to gather together but Gem could tell by their faces that things were hopeless. Without food, without water and without shelter there was no way they could survive. Everything was gone. Some talked of finding another tribe to help but everyone knew that all the other tribes were too far away. Even if they could find another tribe, they would not be welcomed – everyone only just had enough for themselves. Gem looked at the sad and empty eyes of her friends, family and fellow Stargatherers.

She suddenly remembered her great-grandmother's words: "When everything else has gone, use this."

She pulled out the silver box and opened it. Inside, the Wozat seemed to be pulsing gently.

She looked at it for a moment, thinking about what to do. Then she took the Wozat from the box and put it into the sand. She knew, somehow, that this was the right thing to do.

At first nothing happened. Then the Wozat sank into the sand. A few seconds later a tiny shoot pushed its way up and started to grow bigger and bigger. Gem jumped back as it grew faster and faster. The rest of the tribe, noticing

something strange, gathered round and were
stunned to see the Wozat take on the shape of
a house. They were amazed and would have
stood and stared but the house grew bigger
still and they had to move out of the way. New
rooms grew; then courtyards, balconies,
towers, and fountains of pure water. Gardens
with beautiful trees and flowers and vegetables
appeared. Fields and shelters for animals grew
before their eyes, and orchards with many
different fruits sprang up. There was even a
small lake with fish swimming in it.

When the Wozat had finished growing,
there stood a beautiful palace with more than
enough room for everyone.

After standing and staring for quite some
time, the Stargatherers began to explore their
new home. Each family found a part of the
palace that seemed to be made just for them.
In some places there were looms and wheels
for making pottery, kilns and ovens for making
bread. There was a beehive where bees were
already busy making honey, and all sorts of
tools for making and growing things.

Gem found that she had her own place, a room with a balcony that overlooked a gurgling stream. On the bank of that stream stood a beautiful tree, just like the one on the box. Gem would spend many hours looking at that tree and remembering the Wozat.

The years passed but the people of the Stargatherers never forgot about Gem. They told their children and they told their grandchildren about how one girl believed, and how the tiniest of things became the most important.

It's not only on the small blue planet that a tiny seed can produce something amazing! Have you ever picked up a little acorn and then looked up at the massive oak tree it fell from? The tree started as an acorn too, and just grew and grew! Jesus talked about another kind of 'seed' in the Bible. He said that even if people only believe a tiny bit in what God can do, he will still do fantastic things!

"If you had faith no larger than a mustard seed, you could tell this mountain to move from here to there. And it would. Everything would be possible for you."

Matthew 17:20

Cloudburst

Spendthrift was not a very clever man, but he was very rich and important. Remember that: he's important and rich, but not clever.

He lived in a very hot land but he liked to travel. One day Spendthrift was travelling further than he had ever travelled before when he saw something. His toes curled and his eyes opened wide. This thing was amazing. It hung in the sky all white and wispy like a... like a... well, he didn't know what it was like. It was wonderfully, incredibly, totally different.

Under the "thing" stood a man with a pointy hat. It was a bit tatty, but even though the man looked poor, Spendthrift knew he must be very wealthy indeed to own a thing so beautiful, so amazing.

Without asking his name or saying hello, Spendthrift went right up to the man and said,

"How much?"

The man stared at him and said nothing.

Spendthrift had travelled in many lands and knew the art of speaking with people of different languages and so he said, very slowly and very loudly, "HOW MUCH?"

The man tilted his head, narrowed his eyes and quietly replied, "How much for what?"

"For the 'thing'," answered Spendthrift and raised his eyes to the sky.

"What 'thing'?"

"That 'thing'!"

"Which 'thing'?"

"That 'thing'!"

"That 'thing'?"

"That 'thing'!"

"The cloud?"

"Yes, yes, yes, the thing you just said." Spendthrift was feeling very excited.

The man looked at him as if he had turned purple with yellow spots.

"You cannot buy a

cloud! It is impossible, unheard of, quite out of the question and very, very silly." Spendthrift had bought many things in his life and he knew what was going on here. The man was haggling and he wanted more money. What the man obviously did not know was that Spendthrift had lots and lots of money and no matter how much it would cost he was going to buy the "thing". He wrote down a number on a piece of paper; a very large number indeed. He handed it to the man and smiled.

The man looked at the number and his eyes grew very large.

"But you cannot buy a cloud," he croaked.

Spendthrift offered him an even larger number.

The man looked at Spendthrift again and said, very slowly and very loudly, "YOU CANNOT BUY A CLOUD!"

And so it went on. The man tried to explain
to Spendthrift that clouds were not to be
bought and Spendthrift offered larger and
larger numbers. At last the man gave up.

"I give up!" he said.

Spendthrift gave a yell of triumph, weighed
the man down with money and sent
him and his tatty pointy hat
on his way with a couple of
little pushes. He looked up to
the sky and was filled with
joy. It was his, all his. It was
lovely, it was beautiful and it
was his. He did a little
dance; not a very good little
dance but it expressed how he felt. He jumped
up and down, he shouted, he laughed, he cried,
he whooped and he cheered. And then he did
them all again for good measure.

After a while, however, he felt very tired
and decided to sleep. He lay down under his
precious cloud and soon fell fast asleep. In his
dreams he ran through the fields with his
cloud. He and his cloud sat in his garden and
sipped rose tea. They went on journeys
together and he introduced his cloud to the
Sultan of his great home city. He even gave his
cloud a name – Fluffy.

The next morning an approaching traveller awakened him from his slumber. As she drew near, Spendthrift shouted, "Is it not lovely, beautiful, so incredible? And it is all mine."

The traveller looked around and said, "What is?"

"My cloud, my lovely cloud."

"What cloud?"

As we already know, Spendthrift had travelled in many lands and knew the art of speaking with people of different languages and so he said, very slowly and very loudly, "THE CLOUD ABOVE MY HEAD," and he pointed upwards.

The traveller looked up and frowned.

Spendthrift looked up and… his cloud was gone. Frantically he looked around. In the distance, on the horizon, he saw a tiny speck. Without asking her name or saying goodbye (or even "hello" for that matter) Spendthrift left the traveller and ran after his cloud.

"Fluffy! Come back, Fluffy!" he cried as he went.

The traveller, who was called Anneka, watched him for a while and soon was joined by a man in a pointy hat.

"Some people spend a lot of time chasing after things they cannot keep," he said quietly.

Anneka agreed.

* shouldn't that be 'why on a small blue planet'?!!

Why on earth did Spendthrift think he could own a cloud?* Surely he knew that it wasn't really his? Jesus told a story about owning "things".

"A rich man's farm produced a big crop, and he said to himself, 'What can I do? I don't have a place large enough to store everything.'

Later, he said, 'Now I know what I'll do. I'll tear down my barns and build bigger ones, where I can store all my grain and other goods. Then I'll say to myself, "You have stored up enough good things to last for years to come. Live it up! Eat, drink, and enjoy yourself."'

But God said to him, 'You fool! Tonight you will die. Then who will get what you have stored up?'"

Although the man owned a lot, he couldn't own it for ever because he wasn't going to be around for ever.

Luke 12:16–21

The world of Grub

On a rock in the middle of the desert stood Grub. The rock was not very large but for Grub, it was all he knew; it was his entire world. Whichever way Grub looked, all he could see was sand. Sand to the north and sand to the south, sand to the east and sand to the west, sand just about everywhere. So Grub decided that because he could not see anything else, his rock was all there was. Grub's rock was the world.

Each day Grub would take a stroll around his world. It did not take him very long and sometimes he would do two or even three trips around the world. Most of the time he sat and chewed on some of the gimble grass that grew through the cracks in the rock and tried very, very hard not to think about anything – it was simpler that way.

One day as he was nibbling on a particularly sweet piece of gimble grass, a spoot floated by on its yellow balloon.

"Hello," it called and descended until it was quite close to Grub, "are you lost? Do you need some help?"

Grub was confused. "What do you mean?"

"Well, I couldn't help noticing that you were stuck out here in the middle of nowhere and I thought that maybe I could give you a ride somewhere."

"There is nowhere else," said Grub.

"Yes there is," laughed the spoot, "there is a whole world out there full of wonders. Over there," it pointed south, "is a forest full of trees of all shapes and sizes. There are creatures of all different kinds and there is a huge river full of even more creatures. Why not come and see? Some of them are my close personal friends."

Grub looked at the spoot and said, "You are making it all up. You are trying to trick me. There is nowhere else. This is the world. Go away!"

The spoot shrugged, gave a little tug on the string of his balloon and rose into the sky. Soon it disappeared over the horizon.

For a while things went back to normal. Grub walked around his world and soon forgot about his strange visitor. As he got halfway around his world for the second time he saw a cloud of sand coming across the desert. Grub stopped and watched as a small creature approached, riding on the back of a taller one.

"Hello," shouted the small thing, which was in fact a stub mounted on a crested longleg.

Grub pretended not to hear.

"Hello there," the stub shouted louder, "do you need some help? I am going north and if you need a ride I would be glad to help."

"Go away and stop pretending there is anything else out there. This is the world and you do not even exist, so there!" yelled Grub.

"Oh, my dear fellow, on the contrary, there is a whole world of wonders out there, of which I am only one. In the Northlands where

I live are great white beasts as tall as the highest tree, walking mountains and many people who would love to meet such a unique and marvellous creature as yourself," said the stub cheerfully. The longleg just nodded – well, you wouldn't expect a longleg to talk, would you?

"You cannot trick me," said Grub and turned his back on the stub.

"Well, if you are sure old chap, I'll be on my way," sighed the stub and rode away into the distance.

Grub was angry. His simple life was being ruined by things that could not exist, and they were talking to him! Worse than that, he had been having thoughts – yes, thoughts. No matter how he tried, no matter how many times he walked around the world, they kept popping into his head. By the time the next creature came by, Grub was ready. He closed his eyes and put his fingers in his ears. If he had been looking and listening he would have found himself face to face with a trivil. The trivil tried in vain to tell Grub of the wonderful world he was missing, of rainbow waterfalls, cloud shepherds and stardust. The trivil eventually gave up and went on his way. Grub kept his fingers in his ears and his eyes closed for two days, until he got really hungry and had to get himself some gimble grass. He was relieved to see that there were no strange creatures anywhere near his world.

For months nothing happened and Grub had almost managed to forget his visitors, when he saw another plume of sand in the distance. He was about to put his fingers in his ears when he noticed that something was not right. As he watched, his eyes grew rounder

and he started to tremble. It was a tornado and it was heading his way. He looked around but there was nowhere to hide. He clung on to some gimble grass and squeezed his eyes shut. The tornado raced towards him, roaring and screaming until it reached him and plucked him off his rock. Round and round he spun for what seemed like hours… and then nothing.

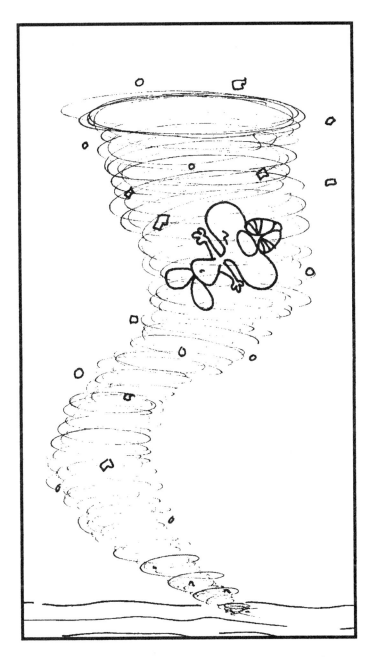

The sound stopped and he felt as if he was floating.

Eventually he opened his eyes and to his amazement he saw below him an emerald forest full of creatures and plants of all shapes and colours, a huge winding river and many things he could not even put a name to. A huge, vibrant, wonderful world.

He looked up and there was the spoot with the yellow balloon smiling down at him.

"Isn't it wonderful?" said the spoot.

Grub just smiled.

The 'Orrible Orange Oogle

"Space. The huge empty bit between things. This is the voyage of the spaceship Aardvark. Its mission? To get from A to B without breaking down. To slowly deliver stuff that people don't really need."

Captain Caruthers stopped recording. He was feeling low. Everything had been going fine until the porridge incident. Who could have guessed that a stray bowl of porridge would cause so much mess? He closed the inspection hatch and looked again at the ship's manual.

"Problems with penguins," he read aloud, "how to wear a wig in zero gravity, our enemy in space – the baked bean."

Nothing, absolutely nothing, on what to do when you've spilt porridge into the main control panel. In fact, there was no mention of porridge at all.

He looked out of the ship's window. Where he was supposed to see lots of nothing, he could see lots of rock but then that is what you should expect when you get porridge in the controls and crash into a small moon!

"It's not that it's a bad moon," he said to no one in particular. "It's quite nice really. I just don't want to spend the rest of my life on it."

He pushed a button and brought up the star chart.

"OK. I was travelling along here and the porridge thing happened here. So I must be... here. The third moon of a planet called Bob. I guess they couldn't be bothered to call it a proper name."

He swivelled on his chair. "Computer?"

"Yes, Captain?" said the calm voice.

"When can we fly again?"

"If we take into account the damage caused by pouring porridge into a place porridge should never be..."

"I didn't pour it, I spilt it," said the Captain defensively.

"And if we take into account that out of over three hundred inhabited planets in this sector you had to hit a tiny lump of rock that is not even on the shipping lanes..."

"It's quite a nice lump of rock though."

Captain Caruthers could feel the computer staring at him.

The computer continued, "And if we also take into account that both engines are damaged beyond repair, I would estimate our time of arrival to be…"

"Yes?"

"…never."

The next day Captain Caruthers was staring at the distant surface of the planet Bob and playing with a hole in his sock, when the computer chimed.

"There is a ship approaching, Captain."

Sure enough, there in the distance, a small ship appeared. It was heading towards them.

"It is an ambulance ship, Captain."

"It must have seen us. Woo-hoo!" yelled the Captain as he stumbled about looking for his left boot. "We're saved!"

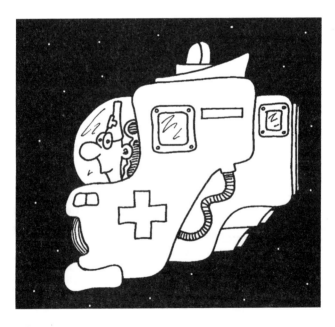

It was indeed an ambulance ship. As it drew near Captain Caruthers could see the doctor flying it. He could see the big red cross on the front, on the side and on the back.

"Wait a minute. He's not stopping!" He started to shout, "Hey! Where are you going? Stop!"

"I do not think he can hear you, Captain," purred the computer.

"But he can see me!" he raged. But for all his shouting the ship still disappeared into the distance.

"I don't even like porridge," he sighed.

"Five hundred and twenty-seven thousand, three hundred and sixty-two?" asked the Captain.

"Nearly," replied the ever-patient computer.

"What? I've counted them three times."

"You missed one."

"Where?"

"Behind the fire extinguisher."

The Captain looked behind the fire extinguisher, "Ha, there you are. Well, that's five hundred and twenty-seven thousand, three hundred and sixty-three rivets in the control room."

"That is correct, Captain. There is also

another ship approaching. A class two breakdown ship."

"At last," the Captain smiled, "they must have got our distress signal. Is it the Space Breakdown Company?"

"Yes, Captain."

Captain Caruthers sat down and watched as the huge ship approached. He could see the big yellow letters that spelled out the name of the company stretching the entire length of the vehicle – Space Breakdown Company. He thought, with satisfaction, of his wise decision two years ago to join their breakdown plan. They guaranteed to get you to anywhere in the galaxy within seven days or your money back. At five hundred credits it was a little expensive but what price could be put on peace of mind?

As they got closer he could see one of the mechanics at the window. He was waving. They got closer still. The Captain pointed to

his Space Breakdown Company membership badge. The mechanic put both thumbs up and smiled. They kept on going.

"Er, just a minute, stop!" shouted the Captain. "I want my money back! Not that it will do me any good stuck on a moon, especially one of three circling a planet called Bob."

"You have been refunded five hundred credits by the Space Breakdown Company," said the computer smoothly.

Captain Caruthers did what any hero would do in this situation: he sulked.

Three days later the Captain was eating a bowl of porridge, and finding that actually it was not that bad. He had never really tried it before and his first bowl had ended up in the delicate electronics, but now he found he quite liked it. Suddenly all the ship's alarms started to sound. Putting the bowl down very carefully he began to try to work out what was wrong. He was not too worried. He could handle anything as long as it was not a huge orange alien.

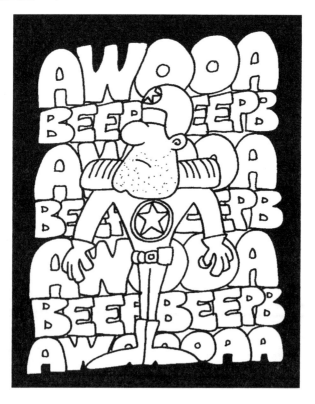

"Captain! There is a huge orange alien approaching," said the computer calmly.

"You're enjoying this, aren't you?"

"I do not know what you mean," replied the computer.

Captain Caruthers was sure the computer was grinning.

"Alien species identified as 'Orrible Orange Oogle."

The 'Orrible Orange Oogle is the scariest, nastiest, most vicious creature in the whole universe, or so it is said. It doesn't need a ship, it just floats through space eating everything in its path. The Captain had read the books and he had seen the videos. He stopped for a moment to consider their situation.

"We're doomed," he whispered.

The 'Orrible Orange Oogle came closer and closer until he could see the whites of its many eyes. Closer still. It opened its mouth and the Captain closed his eyes.

"Having a spot of bother?" it said.

The Captain opened his eyes and his mouth followed.

"I think I can help," it continued.

Long orange arms stretched out from the side of the Oogle. It picked up the ship very gently, and carefully carried it to the nearest space station.

"There you go," it said, "you should be OK now."

"Er… thank you," said the Captain shakily.

Captain Caruthers thought the Oogle was quite nice, not 'orrible at all. They had a long chat. It turned out the Oogle's name was Nigel.

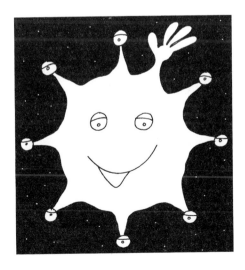

There are no 'Orrible Orange Oogles in it though. Pssst… it might help you to know that samaritan people were outcasts!

91

Small blue planet quiz

1 What is Hal's full name?

2 What kind of tree did Hal climb?

3 How many different kinds of
bloopers are mentioned in 'One of
our bloopers is missing'?

4 Who looked after the
bloopers?

5 What colour is Bik?

6 What colour are Bok's
pyjamas?

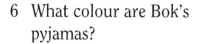

7 What are the names of the
   four groundlings in the race?

8 What does the little ™ mean on
   Spike's Dynamo™ shoes?

9 How many crocodiles did Hector take
   to see the king?

10 Who visited Hector's house?

11 What was carved on the lid of Gem's small
   silver box?

12 What was the name of Gem's
   tribe?

13 Spendthrift met a man. What shape
   was his hat?

14 What did Spendthrift call his cloud?

15 What colour was the spoot's balloon?

16 What kind of creature was the stub riding?

17 According to the ship's manual what is 'our enemy in space'?

18 What was the 'Orrible Orange Oogle's name?

Answers!

1 Halbonbaltiddlyaljofal

2 Findle tree

3 9 (*What other kinds of bloopers do you think there might be?*)

4 E!

5 Bright yellow

6 Pink

7 Beaky, Pebble, Spike and Izzy

8 Trademark

9 23

10 A little country mouse

11 A tree

12 The Stargatherers

13 Pointy

14 Fluffy

15 Yellow

16 A crested longleg

17 The baked bean

18 Nigel